PEOPLE SKILLS: STUDENT BOOK

Textbook and On the Job Training Manual

From DTR Inc.'s Work Readiness Certification Series for the second edition of People Skills

JAY GOLDBERG

The opinions expressed in this manuscript are solely the opinions of the author and do not represent the opinions or thoughts of the publisher. The author represents and warrants that he either owns or has the legal right to publish all material in this book.

This book was written to help individuals understand and improve their employability knowledge and skills. The information detailed in the book is based on the experience, knowledge and observations of Jay Goldberg. Since hiring, firing, and promoting employees varies by company and the person performing the task, there is no guarantee by the author or publisher, expressed or implied that following everything in this book will result in a job, not getting fired, or an increase in compensation; or that employees that read this book will implement what they learn and become exceptional employees.

PEOPLE SKILLS
Textbook and On the Job Training Manual

From DTR Inc.'s Work Readiness Certification Series

Workplace Basics
Workplace Skills
People Skills
Customer Service

Contact the author, via email, at Book@DTRConsulting.BIZ. Please type "your work readiness book" in the subject line of the email to ensure that your email is not deleted as junk mail.

To order more books go to www.createspace.com/5531805

ISBN - 978-1514147054

Table of Contents

Communication Skills

Communication refers to both verbal and nonverbal communication. What you say and how you say it is very important. I remember a Seinfeld episode where Kramer had a line in a Woody Allen movie. The line was "These pretzels are making me thirsty." Each of the four main characters has their own spin on how the line should be said, and based on how the character says the line, the emotion communicated to the listener changes. From matter of fact, to the appearance of great thirst, to severe annoyance, to anger at the pretzels; the message communicated changed based on the delivery of the line.

Likewise you can get messages across just by your actions. For good examples, watch an old Marx Brothers movie or catch Penn and Teller's act. In both cases there is a person who does not talk, but gets across what he is thinking just on his actions and facial expressions.

Verbal communication

Being able to communicate with your co-workers, supervisors, and customers is a workplace skill that is valued by employers. Therefore, do not use slang, computer lingo, or street talk when talking or writing. For example, using computer lingo, if I finished talking to you and then said, "TTYL", you may or may not know that I meant that I'll "talk to you later." Worse, what if I wrote you a note and started it, "IMHO", and then went on to contradict what you wrote me. You might get the impression that I was correcting you rather than just stating my views on the subject ("IMHO" means 'in my humble opinion"). Also, if one of your co-workers is provoking you and your supervisor comes over to ask you what is going on, don't say, "I was chillin' when my homey came over and started fronting." Just say, "I wasn't doing anything when Bob came over and started provoking me." Obviously you should also avoid slang that many will take offense too, even if you do not believe you are using it in an offensive manner.

When communicating verbally in the workplace, speak clearly, and choose your words carefully. There are other things to remember while communicating in the workplace. Including:

1. Don't take how people react personally. Their reactions are usually about the impact of what you communicated, and not directed towards you personally. For example, if you had to communicate to a co-worker that your supervisor said everyone had to work late, his/her response may be angry, but the anger is at the situation and is not directed at you.

2. Do not make up facts, or even guess at facts. If you do not know an answer, just say so.

3. If you are unsure of what someone means, don't assume, ask questions until it becomes clear to you.

4. Be patient. Often someone you are talking too will be saying something you already know. Allow that person the opportunity to say what he or she wants so that he or she can have the satisfaction of knowing that he or she was heard.

5. Be open to other people's points of view. Everyone has different life experiences. Do not automatically discount other people's opinions. You just may find that others have interesting perspectives worth thinking about.

6. Understand that the person you are conveying information to may have difficulties that arise from your discussion. Do not downplay something that the person you are speaking to may find difficult regarding what is being discussed. Instead, acknowledge it, and then offer suggestions to help ease their pain.

7. Avoid arguments. Concentrate on what you and the other party agree on first, to establish common ground, and then move towards solving differences. Be understanding of everyone's position in the discussion by looking at the situation from the other person's point of view.

8. Be sure to listen to what others are saying, do not step on their words or tune them out.

9. When using examples, personalize the examples so that it is easier for the other party to relate to what you are saying.

Verbal communication worksheet

Understanding your communication strengths and weaknesses is the first step towards becoming an effective communicator in all scenarios. Use the worksheet that follows to indicate your strengths, weaknesses and a plan to improve your overall communication skills.

1. Which three of the nine communication skills listed previously are your strengths (write the number)

________ ________ ________

2. Which three of the nine communication skills listed previously do you need to work on, or be aware of, the most (write the number)

________ ________ ________

3. How do you plan to improve, or be more aware of, the three areas you indicated in question 2?

____
____
____
____
____
____
____
____
____

Non-verbal communication

One of my favorite books is *Dune* by Frank Herbert. Besides being a fascinating story, an aspect I found very interesting was the communication between characters in political situations. Besides the dialog, Frank Herbert also sets up the scenes by writing about the personal signals involved in many of those interactions.

Believe it or not (George isn't at home, where could I be - sorry, that tune just sticks in my head from George's answering machine in a Seinfeld episode), *Dune* opened my eyes to reading the motivation behind personal signals at work. I was fresh out of graduate school with my MBA working on a project in the Systems and Technology Department for the Merchant Credit Card Division of Citibank. There was an Assistant Vice President (AVP), who was not in charge of the area, who, at times, would come to work in a t-shirt with a sweat stain. Now, this was a conservative bank, at a time when everyone showed up in suits and ties. This AVP was not a slob, was not unsophisticated, and was not unaware of how he should dress. So using my new found "Dune" skills, I figured out what his purpose was in coming to work on occasion in a t-shirt with a sweat stain. He was saying nonverbally, "If I can show up like this to work and get away with it, I'm very important to management and not someone you should ever cross."

Now, I do not recommend you try this at your place of employment; this was an extremely rare situation.

As an aside, one day I asked the AVP if he ever read *Dune*, and he said a very energetic, "Yes, it's one of my favorite books."

Now I'll go on to the topic. Be aware of the personal signals you are broadcasting. You may say the right thing but if your body language is saying something else, you will be sending mixed signals. You can also use those always present personal signals to your advantage. By reading the personal signals of the individual you are talking too, you can tell if he/she comprehends what you just told him/her. A puzzled look goes a long way in letting you know you will have to find different words to explain what you just said again. I do that all the time when I teach my entrepreneurship course. If I see looks of acknowledgement, I go on to the next topic, on the rare occasion I see some looks of confusion, I go over the topic again, presenting it in a different way.
Personal signals

Below are some personal signals and what they generally indicate when communicating with others. Despite television shows like *Lie to Me,* I do not believe this is an exact science, so consider what follows as a rule of thumb more than a given.

- ✓ Direct eye contact, but not staring (shows interest)
- ✓ Long stare without head movement (annoyance)
- ✓ Rolling of eyes (frustration)
- ✓ Avoiding eye contact (uncomfortable, wants situation to end)
- ✓ Winking (friendly acknowledgement)
- ✓ Tight lipped smile (hiding something)
- ✓ Normal laugh (relaxed)
- ✓ Forced laugh (nervous cooperation)
- ✓ Teeth grinding (tension)
- ✓ Biting lip (tension)
- ✓ Hand over mouth (suppressing something)
- ✓ Nodding yes (agreement)
- ✓ Head shaking no (disagreement)
- ✓ Looking down (disinterested)
- ✓ Slight tilt of head (shows you are listening)
- ✓ Head tilted down (criticism)
- ✓ Chin up (pride)
- ✓ Slow head nodding (listening intently)
- ✓ Fast head nodding (agree, get on with it already)
- ✓ Crossed arms (defensive)
- ✓ Leaning forward (shows interest)
- ✓ Leaning back (to reflect and take time to think)
- ✓ Leaning on chin (shows concentration)
- ✓ Cupping chin (boredom)
- ✓ Clasp hands behind neck or body (extreme confidence)
- ✓ One hand on back of neck (disagreement)
- ✓ Grasping upper arms (insecure)
- ✓ Palms up (submissive)
- ✓ Palms down (in control)

- ✓ Pointing finger at someone (aggression)
- ✓ Clenched fists (determined resistance)
- ✓ Interwoven clenched fingers (negativity)
- ✓ Rubbing hands (anticipation)
- ✓ Hands in pockets (disinterest)
- ✓ Constantly shifting position (not relaxed)
- ✓ Stroking nose (exaggeration, possibly lying)
- ✓ Scratching neck (disbelief)
- ✓ Yawning (fatigue)
- ✓ Scowling (anger)
- ✓ Tapping fingers (impatience)

In addition to using these personal signals to read your audience, know how others may be interpreting you when you use some of these personal signals.

Personal signals (nonverbal communication) worksheet

1. Understanding the personal signals you use, often naturally without even thinking about what you are doing can go a long way to ensuring that the personal signals you actually use in the workplace match the message you are communicating and convey how you truly feel about the situation. Use the worksheet that follows to indicate three personal signals (use the prior list of personal signals) you know you use appropriately to help you convey what you are saying or feeling.

1. ____
2. ____
3. ____

2. Now list two personal signals that you use that seem to come up automatically and often get you into trouble because they either convey the wrong message or give away what you are

feeling in a situation where that is inappropriate and may get you into trouble despite your words.

1. ____
2. ____

Obviously, these are two personal signals you need to be aware of and try to eliminate.

EXERCISE PS1

Robots for Ronnie Inc. (RFR Inc.) is a growing management consulting company in the field of Robotics. While the company has an excellent reputation in the area of using robotics to solve manufacturing problems, the staff has problems communicating with its customers. To help solve these problems, RFR Inc. hires you to observe staff communications with customers. What follows are the first four communication sessions you observe. Indicate whether or not these sessions represented good or bad communication skills and then explain why you choose good or bad. (FYI - "Robots for Ronnie" is a song by Crack the Sky)

Q1. The Senior Vice President (SVP) of RFR Inc. wants to know what customers think of their new Robot, Model ABC. The SVP asks an employee to obtain feedback from customers on how well the robot is doing in their places of business. The employee asks the following to ten customers, "Could you please tell me about your experience with Robot ABC?" The employee does his/her homework and knows exactly what the robot is being used for at each of the ten businesses and adds a specific comment to the end of the question. When a client responds with a bad experience, since the employee knows what the robot is being used for, the employee acknowledges the customer's difficulty, and helps the customer overcome their issues.

Q2. An employee is given the task to inform a group of sales representatives about Robot Model ABC. The employee was up all night working. The presentation starts at 7:30 AM the next morning. During the presentation, the employee gets across all important details of Robot ABC, including its features, uses, and why it is better than the competition's similar model. The presentation was given very straight forward with little to no emotion, a few yawns, and at times was delivered very slowly.

Q3. An employee is asked to give a presentation of how Robot Model ABC functions at a convention of Powdered Metal Manufacturing Plant owners and managers. This employee has excellent presentation skills, and knows the product very well. Throughout the presentation the employee uses examples of how the robot can be used. All of the examples are long and very detailed. The examples are in the medical and theme park (e.g. Disneyland) industries. There were no powdered metal examples.

Q4. On day three of your assignment, there is a recall of Robot Model XYZ. An employee is placed in charge of picking up the customers robots. When a client asks the employee why the robot is being recalled, the employee stares at the client a long time (head held still), then points a finger at the client and says, "Call customer service, they can give you the details.

*****

Getting Along with Co-Workers

Here is a recommendation I trust you will follow; treat your co-workers like "friendly neighbors."

When you move into a new neighborhood, your neighbors are already there. You don't choose them and you have no power on how long they will remain your neighbors. The same is true in the workplace. When you get a new job, there are already people employed by the company. You don't choose them, and you have no power on how long they will stay with the company. Your best strategy is to get along with all your co-workers. If you do, you will be a positive force in your workplace, and that goes a long way on increasing your value to your employer. It also shows that you can get along with all kinds of people, which demonstrates that you have the ability to manage diverse teams of employees. Therefore, getting along with your co-workers is not only the ethical (right) thing to do, it is the smart thing to do to increase your job security, and keep you in the running for supervisory positions.

Blueprint for getting along with co-workers

If you keep in mind the concept "friendly neighbors" you'll be okay. The best strategy with neighbors is not to get too personal, and that is true with your co-workers.

(1) Leave "water cooler talk" to what was on television last night, not what you heard your co-worker did last night. Gossip is usually wrong, and often hurtful to the person being discussed. Keep away from office gossip, and if you hear something, certainly, do not pass it on. It is possible that your co-worker will consider gossip about him/her harassment. Worst case he/she could consider it a hostile workplace. If your co-worker talks to his/her supervisor, or the Human Resources Department, you don't want to be part of the group that gets called on the carpet to explain the situation. You definitely don't want to be the center of the "gossip storm." If you are a "gossip-hound", stand in line at the supermarket, read the headlines of the magazines that line the aisles, and gossip about celebrities at the water cooler. Don't cross the line no matter how tempting, and spread gossip and rumors about your co-workers.

(2) Don't get dragged into your co-workers' personal problems, and don't share your personal problems with your co-workers. If your co-workers start to talk to you about something too personal, just say, "I'm sorry to hear that. I'm sure you'll be fine." Then get back to work. Asking questions and expanding on the comments will just lead to more details and future conversations. The same goes for you. Separate your friends from your friendly co-workers and keep your conversations about your personal problems to the people that care about you; your friends.

(3) If a co-worker is complaining about work, don't join in. You would be surprised what is overheard and gets back to management. Instead say something like, "I know you're going through a tough time now, but I believe in you and you're going to be fine." In general be positive and supportive, not negative or a "Doubting Thomas" or a "constant complainer."

(4) If a co-worker is doing something wrong on the job and it is negatively impacting the quality of the work, don't allude to it; don't talk behind his/her back. You have to be discreet and direct. One approach is to say, "I have been doing <that function> differently, can you show me how you have been doing it." After he/she shows you, explain how you have been doing it. Hopefully it will become clear that your way is the proper way and your co-worker will change. If your co-worker continues to perform <that function> incorrectly, inform him/her that you will be talking to your supervisor to clear up the proper way to complete <that function>. Then tell your supervisor how you have been doing <that function> and ask if it is correct. If your supervisor informs you that it is correct, say that some of your other co-workers are not performing the task that way and may need a refresher in how the procedure is done. Then leave the next move up to your supervisor.

Notice how there was no arguing with your co-worker on how <that function> should be done. Also, you approached your co-worker to verify the way you were performing <that function>. Finally, you told your co-worker that you were going to talk to your supervisor (not going behind a co-worker's back), and you approached your supervisor to help clarify a job function for yourself, not to discuss how your co-worker was performing <that function>.

(5) Do not take credit for something another co-worker does. When you do a good job and it is recognized, take full credit. If you do something as a team and are given credit, share the credit with your team members. If you get credit for something that someone else did, shine the light on your co-worker. Believe it or not ("George isn't at home" - there goes that song from Seinfeld in my head again, sorry). Let me start again, believe it or not you will score big points for being honest. A supervisor values an employee he/she can trust. Supervisors

also value an employee that can share credit with team members.

(6) Don't be overbearing. You may have done things differently in your old job, or you may have liked the way the workplace was run better in a previous job, or you may not like the way a new supervisor is running things. Do not keep talking about the way things used to be. Accept change. However, if you truly believe you can identify ways to improve the workplace, arrange a meeting with your supervisor and talk to him/her about it. But do not preach or complain to your co-workers, and accept the final decision your supervisor makes.

(7) Treat your co-workers like team members, not competitors. That means helping them when needed, and not being afraid to ask for help when you need it. When asking for help, be sure you ask the right person. The person you ask needs to be an expert in the area in which you need help. If you ask the 12th ranked salesperson for help with your sales technique, you may not get the best answers. The person to ask is the top ranked salesperson. Remember, if a co-worker teaches you something incorrectly, that is not an excuse for doing something the wrong way in your supervisor's eyes, unless, of course, your supervisor told you to ask that person for help. After receiving help, be sure to thank your co-worker for his/her help.

(8) Perform your job functions well. In most workplaces employees' job functions are dependent on the work of others. Therefore, if you do not perform your job functions timely and accurately, it could make it difficult for some of your co-workers to perform their job functions timely and accurately. Then, depending upon the management style in the workplace, even though you might be the cause for the below-par performance of others, management could hold everybody accountable. You could be directly impacting the compensation

and career growth of some of your co-workers. So performing your job well not only is important to the business, and to you; but also to your co-workers who rely on your work. So if you are making mistakes on the job, and your co-workers become annoyed with you, do not get angry thinking they are getting involved in something that is solely your business; it is their business as well.

(9) Be even-keeled at work because you will be dealing with a wide range of people. This is not just the obvious of dealing with people of varying religions, races, ethnicity, sexual orientation, gender, age, disabilities, etc.; but also dealing with people with varying personalities, values, political views, and outlooks on life. Work is not the place to get into heated discussions or to show your prejudices (which you shouldn't have anyway). So avoid conversations on those heated political conversations and polarizing topics with your co-workers.

EXERCISE PS2

Jack works with and lives next door next to Juliet and Sawyer. Last night he heard loud talking coming from Juliet and Sawyer's home, looked out his window, and saw Juliet leaving in a huff and driving off. Jack gets into work two hours earlier than Juliet. When he got up the next morning, Juliet's car is not in her driveway. Later in the day Kate, a woman Jack has a crush on, approaches Jack and says "Juliet is in a bad mood today, I wonder if she is having problems at home with Sawyer?"

Q1. How should Jack answer that question?

Because of the Holiday rush, Hugo has been working very hard, including long hours and little time for breaks. His buddy and co-worker, Charley, stands up, throws his hands in the air, and says, "This is bull. I need a break and I'm taking a break." In the room there are lots of head nods and a few others get up to walk to the vending machines with Charlie. As he is leaving, Charlie turns to Hugo and says, "Come on Hugo, don't you agree this is bull? Let's go."

Q2. How should Hugo answer that question? Should Hugo go on break with the others?

Desmond has been the top-rated employee at Lost Island, Inc. for the last three years. He is the only one who knows how to punch the numbers into the Keeping Things Right Machine. Desmond has his eye on a promotional opportunity and believes it is his knowledge of the Keeping Things Right Machine that will eventually get him that promotion. His main competitor for the promotion is Ben. Ben finishes all his assignments early and his supervisor told him he could go home and still get paid for the day. Instead, Ben approaches Desmond and asks him if he can teach him how to punch in the numbers. Desmond is just about to punch in the numbers, so the timing is perfect.

Q3. What should Desmond do?

Jin believes strongly in alternative energy, particularly solar energy (energy from the Sun). Locke, on the other hand has relatives that work in the petroleum industry. Jin and Locke eat lunch together in the employee cafeteria. There are not friends outside of work, but enjoy eating lunch together. Today, Jin gives a speech about the evils of petroleum, the benefits of solar energy, and invites Locke to a rally that is taking place on the weekend, when neither is scheduled to work. Jin has no idea that Locke has relatives that work in the petroleum industry.

Q4. How should Jin respond to Locke's request?

Claire worked very long and hard on a study that is going to be included in the department's monthly report. In the monthly report all information is included as one write-up from the department with no names attached to the individual studies in the report. While putting the report together Claire asks Sayid if he could provide her with some data from his work area. Sayid runs the numbers and hands them to Claire. Claire then analyzes the data, finds some interesting trends, and includes some insightful written analysis in her study. After the department's monthly report is published, the President of the company walks past Sayid's desk, stops, and says, "Sayid, that was a great analysis of your numbers, keep up the good work and you'll go places in this company."

Q5. How should Sayid respond?

*****

Teamwork

The sum of the parts is greater than the whole. That statement is more than just an old wives' tale. It is true. That is why teamwork is important for all businesses. If everyone is working together, then any problem in the workplace is a problem that is important to all workers. Yes, even you. And solutions to problems can come from any worker.

Therefore, to be a valuable employee, look at your place of work as your team, and your co-workers as your teammates. Do what you can to support your teammates and to ensure that your team wins. In this case, winning means the business is making profits by satisfying its customers, thus keeping everyone employed.

Working with the Team Leader

The Team Leader can be a unique person for employees to deal with. When the Team Leader is a supervisor, then the lines of command are obvious. However, often a co-worker will be put in charge of a team. When that happens, you suddenly find yourself having to follow the lead of an individual who is not in charge of your pay raises or your performance review. In fact, this could be someone who has less experience than you, or is at a lower pay scale that you. That doesn't matter. A team needs a leader to be successful and that co-worker was chosen to lead. For the tasks related to the team, you <u>must</u> treat that co-worker as your supervisor. If you do not, it is you who will look bad, not the Team Leader. This is not sports. The Coach (Team Leader) will not get fired if the team does not succeed, and the Owner (Supervisor) can fire the players (workers) rather than Coach (Team Leader) for the team's failure.

If you find yourself in the role of Team Leader, the following will help you be a successful Team Leader:

1. Set goals for the team
2. Provide all team members with a chance to state his/her ideas
3. Get feedback on the ideas presented from the team members
4. Choose the best ideas yourself after hearing all comments, but make it appear as a group choice
5. Assign roles for all team members so they know what to do
6. Use the word "we" when talking about the team, not "I"
7. Recognize individuals for their ideas and accomplishments
8. Whenever possible, do not force individuals who do not get along to pair up; split them up
9. Do not be hesitant to take control; that is your job
10. Take your role seriously; do not kid around with your friends on the team, if you do others may not take you seriously

Another important fact is that Team Leaders get credit for team accomplishments, and they deserve that credit. Managers in baseball, don't hit, don't pitch, and don't field, but get credit when the team wins by putting their players in a position to succeed. It is the same with Team Leaders. Even if the Team Leader's contributions to the work seem to be minimal, the Team Leader ran his/her team in a way that good solutions and work was produced. That is valuable to employers; is recognized; and deserves to be recognized. Despite what people think, not everybody can manage the New York Yankees and win because of their big payroll and star players. Sometimes handling the best of the best is more difficult than rallying a group of highly-motivated over-achievers.

Of course good Team Leaders will share the recognition with his/her team members and note individuals who made major contributions by name. However, that is out of your control. Know that the Team Leader's supervisor understands that the Team Leader could not be successful without contributions from his/her team, and will look at the Team Leader's lack of sharing recognition for the team's accomplishments with his/her team members as a negative. A good supervisor will not show that to the Team Leader's team members, because that would undermine the Team Leader; but know that the greedy Team Leader is not fooling anyone, and is most likely, being chastised or "coached-up" for that behavior behind the scenes.

Team leader skills worksheet

Understanding your team leader skill strengths and weaknesses is the first step towards becoming an effective team leader. Use the worksheet that follows to indicate your strengths, weaknesses and a plan to improve your overall team leader skills.

1. Which three of the ten team leader skills listed previously are your strengths (write the number)

__________ __________ __________

2. Which three of the ten team leader skills listed previously do you need to work on, or be aware of; the most (write the number) __________ __________ __________

3. How do you plan to improve, or be more aware of, the three areas you indicated in question 2?

____

____

____

____

____

How to be a good team member

I am a big proponent of playing team sports. When a team wins a championship, everybody feels good, from the star of the team to the last player off the bench. The Super Bowl MVP (most valuable player) may get to go to Disneyland, but the guy who only played one play gets the championship ring as well.

You don't have to be the star to enjoy it when your team wins.

Therefore, the key to being a good team member at work is to understand your role, do it the best of your ability, help your teammates, ask for help when you need it, treat all team members and the Team Leader with respect, make accomplishing the goal of the team important to you, and feel good about your team's accomplishments no matter what your role was in helping the team reach its goals.

Being a good team player is important to management. Often, talented workers are not good team players and that holds them back from advancing in their careers. The worker that needs to be the center of attention, have the spotlight always shinning on him/her, always has to get his/her way, etc.; is not an ideal employee even if he/she is brilliant in those circumstances. Your workplace is like baseball or football, not golf or tennis. You do not work in a vacuum. You work with others and have to be a good team player, sometimes leading (when given the responsibility to do so by your supervisor), but more often being a good follower.

Value of Diversity in the Workplace

Since the workplace is based on teamwork, the more diversified the team members, the stronger the team.

If a team has team members who can look at a challenge from a variety of backgrounds and viewpoints, the team stands a better chance of coming up with solutions that address all aspects of that challenge.

This includes a mix of workers of different genders, age, ethnicity, race, sexual orientation, etc. The company wants to do business with all customers. If a team is assembled to fix a problem, it is best if the people working on the solution can fairly represent the company's customers.

For that reason, companies that employ a large staff, often have a goal of assembling a diversified workforce. Many ill-advised workers may feel the diversification is due to pressure from forces outside the company. That is a foolish viewpoint. Workplace diversification is strength for a business.

Personal teamwork worksheet

Below are nine positive attitudes that are important for teamwork. Rank them in order from 1 to 9. Use one for your strongest attribute and nine for your weakest attribute. Use each number only once.

Positive attitude	**Rank**
Work well with others	________
Take pride in team accomplishments	________
Provide team spirit	________
Deal with team members openly and honestly	________
Keeps all agreements, is very trustworthy	________
Help team members to get to know each other	________
Good at resolving conflicts between team members	________
Keep the team leader well informed	________
Accepts change easily	________

When working on a team project, remember your strengths and use them; and be aware of your weaker areas and manage them.

EXERCISE PS3

This is a teamwork exercise with no correct answer, as long as your team's answer makes logical and business sense. Arguments could be made for different combinations of answers. In order to pass this exercise you must participate in the team discussion, follow the appointed team leader's rules for running the team respectfully, participate in the team's oral presentation, show interest throughout the team exercise, and demonstrate with your words and personal signals that you are on board with the team leader's final decision. If you are not doing this exercise in a group, and just reading along, think about what you would choose and how you would respond if the team leader went in a different direction.

You work for a very profitable business in the medical research industry. While in the past the company has had some public relations issues in the form of protests; overall the drugs developed by the company has saved tens of thousands of lives.

Past protests have run the gamut from the high price for the company's drugs when they first hit the market, to the use of animals in research, to making the company's drugs more readily available to people in need in poor countries, to not concentrating on developing cures for diseases that are not widespread such as Creutzfeldt-Jakob Disease and Collagen Disorder, to not helping with U.S. unemployment because the company has its production facility overseas.

To help with the bad press, and because the company is a socially conscience enterprise, it has decided to start a working Not for Profit Corporation (a business that does work, not a foundation that gives money to other not for profits). You have been selected as part of team to help decide what area the not for profit should work in, and what three tasks that not for profit should staff up to undertake. The only parameter that senior management has placed on the group is that the not for profit needs to be in an area from one of the recent protests.

Before the team leader is announced, senior management distributes the form that follows and asks each team member to write down his or her initial thoughts, to help start the group discussion. So you fill out the form.

Area for the Not for Profit Corporation (circle one):

A) Helping low income individuals and families in the United States be able to afford new drugs

B) Helping animals

C) Helping people in foreign countries get needed drugs

D) Helping people with rare incurable diseases

E) Helping the local economy

For the area you choose, list three specific tasks the Not for Profit Corporation can perform.

1. ______________________________
____

2. ______________________________
____

3. ______________________________
____

After completing this task, senior management assigns a team leader. The team leader is responsible for choosing the final decision for the area for Not for Profit Corporation and the three tasks that the Not for Profit will undertake. The team leader opens the floor up for discussion …

After the team discussion, the team leader makes the final decision regarding the area and three specific tasks. The team leader then organizes the presentation that will be made to management (instructor) making sure every team member has a role in that presentation.

*****

EXERCISE PS4 (NASA Teamwork Exercise)

There is a fairly well know NASA exercise that is used in employee and classroom teamwork training. Below is the exercise. While there are real answers and they will be presented after the conclusion of the team presentations, you will not be graded on whether or not you get the answers right. However, for classrooms with more than one team, the teams should compete with each other for fun. The team that gets the top three items according to NASA wins the championship. If there is a tie, the team that has the lowest number after adding the ranks of their eight items is the champion.

Like the previous team exercise, in order to pass this exercise you must participate in the team discussion, participate in the team's oral presentation, show interest throughout the team exercise, and demonstrate with your words and personal signals that you are on board with the team's final decisions. ***You will be observed throughout the entire exercise including how you react after the real answers are disclosed.*** *Remember, this is a presentation being made in the workplace; act accordingly throughout. In addition, you will also be judged on the method the team chooses to select the answers and you must present a logical reason for each item chosen in your answer.*

Scenario:

You are a member of a space crew originally scheduled to rendezvous with a mother ship on the lighted surface of the moon. However, due to mechanical difficulties, your ship was forced to land at a spot some 200 miles from the rendezvous point. During reentry and landing, much of the equipment aboard was damaged and, since survival depends on reaching the mother ship, the most critical items available must be chosen for the 200-mile trip.

What follows are the 15 items left intact and undamaged after landing (continues on next page). As a group you must decide on eight items to take with you. However, if you leave out any of the three most important items according NASA (space agency) you all die.

Get busy you have to be on your way in 30 minutes!

_______ Box of matches
_______ Food concentrate
_______ 50 feet of nylon rope
_______ Parachute silk
_______ Portable heating unit
_______ Two .45 caliber pistols
_______ One case of dehydrated milk
_______ Two 100 lb. tanks of oxygen
_______ Stellar map (map of the stars)
_______ Self-inflating life raft
_______ Magnetic compass
_______ 5 gallons of water
_______ Signal flares
_______ First aid kit, including injection needle
_______ Solar-powered FM receiver-transmitter

Assignment:

Decide on a method for selecting the 8 items that allows everyone's opinion to be heard in the short time frame.

Finalize your list of 8 items. Indicate which three items in your list you believe are NASA's top three items.

When called upon, present your results. Everyone in the group must have a role in the oral presentation. Include the following in your presentation:

Method used to decide which items to take.
The 8 items you are taking with your reasoning why.
The 3 items the group thinks were NASA's top three.

*****

Meeting Supervisors' Expectations

For those of you who have forgotten the definition of congruent, it goes like this: if A is the same size as B; and B is the same size as C; then A has to be the same size as C (or A is congruent to C).

At work I have proved in the section, Workplace Basics, that what's good for the business is good for you (more profits, more job security and more money available for employee salaries). It is the same with your supervisor. What is good for the business is good for your supervisor. Therefore, using the congruent theory, what is good for your supervisor is good for you.

In short, your boss <u>wants</u> you to succeed. Your boss is on your side, even if it does not appear that way to you. The better you perform in your job, the better it is for your boss, and the better it is for the business.

This concept works on many different levels.

- ✓ Your supervisor wants you to succeed because your failures are his/her responsibility.

- ✓ Your supervisor wants you to succeed because if you fail and have to be let go, he/she will have to spend valuable time training a new employee and have to accept a learning curve for that new employee, which will reduce productivity (work output). And it is the supervisor who will be held accountable for any work that is not getting done on time.

✓ Your supervisor wants you to succeed because a large part of his/her job is getting you (and your co-workers) to succeed, and if he/she cannot, he/she risks getting a poor performance appraisal and a lower than hoped for raise.

✓ These are in addition to the basic premise that the better everyone performs at work, the more profits the business earns, the more secure the supervisor's job is, and the more money available for supervisor salaries.

Workers who believe that their boss is "out to get them", are either wrong, or have to take a look in the mirror. From the first two sections, Workplace Basics and Workplace Skills, you are aware that even if you are excellent in your job functions, that is not enough to be considered an asset (a plus) in the workplace. Workplace behavior is important. In fact, poor workplace behavior is the biggest cause of a worker who is performing his/her work very well, feeling like his/her boss is "out to get him/her." If you are good at your job and an asset in the workplace, your supervisor will like you.

For example, if you do your job extremely well but are at the center of workplace gossip, or constantly complain about the company to co-workers, or show up late often, or date and dump your co-workers, or tell inappropriate jokes, or forget to leave your personal problems at the door; you will have problems with your supervisor. Something like this is usually going on when workers feel that their boss is picking on them.

Workers look at one item, completed work. Supervisors look at the big picture. Keep in mind that in addition to managing the work produced by his/her staff; it is a supervisor's job to manage the workplace to ensure that there are no problems, and that everyone feels comfortable enough to produce to the best of their abilities. Again, this is not something your supervisor chooses to do; it is not a power trip; it is part of his/her job. Your supervisor is being paid to ensure that the workplace operates smoothly. If it is not operating smoothly, he/she could receive a poor performance appraisal, and a lower than hoped for pay raise; even if all work is completed on time and is of high quality.

EXERCISE PS5

Answer the following questions, good cause for concern or not really a cause for concern regarding the following situations between a worker and a supervisor. If you answer good cause for concern, please explain why.

A company employs 200 phone representatives. Worker A is one of the top 20 phone representatives (in the top 10%) in terms of job performance. At the lunch for the top phone representatives, Worker A meets, and then starts dating Worker B who was also one of the top 20. After a month Worker A starts dating Worker C who was also one of the top 20 phone representatives. Feeling uncomfortable, Worker B immediately finds a new job and quits the company. While dating Worker C, Worker A is flirting with Worker D, another of the top 20 phone representatives. After their last discussion, Worker A gets the feeling that the Phone Center Supervisor may not be on his or her side.

Q1. Cause for concern? Yes Not really If yes, why?

Worker A is the highest rated employee in the top rated department in the Company. Worker A is also a Miami Dolphins fan. Worker B is a New York Jets fan. Last night on Monday night football the Dolphins beat the Jets to get into the playoffs while also knocking the Jets out of the playoffs. Worker A comes to work and good naturedly teases Worker B about the Dolphins defeating the Jets. The Supervisor witnesses this short, good natured exchange. Later, Worker A finds out that the Supervisor is a big-time New York Jets fan. Suddenly, Worker A starts worrying if he/she has done damage to his/her career.

Q2. Cause for concern? Yes Not really If yes, why?

*****

Supervisor responsibilities

A supervisor's responsibilities on the job are many. You need to understand that your supervisor is being paid to manage and direct you. Supervisors delegate work to his/her staff, not by seniority, not by which worker he/she likes or dislikes. It is not personal. Your supervisor delegates and splits up work by how he/she believes the overall work he/she is responsible for will get completed best. Your supervisor is not only responsible for his/her work, but is responsible for your work, and your co-workers' work as well.

This may mean that some of your co-workers, who are not as efficient as you, seem to get the easier assignments. That is not because your supervisor likes them better and favors them with an easy work day. It is because he/she feels that that is the assignment that best fits their skills. Supervisors look at giving tough assignments to an employee as a badge of honor for that employee, not a punishment. If your supervisor did not think you could handle the tougher work assignment, you would not get it. After all, your supervisor is responsible for that work as well. This also means that you are thought of more highly in the company and will, most likely, get higher raises, and have a better chance at a promotion. By the way, workers exaggerate about salaries and raises. So if a co-worker tells you he/she got a raise and it was higher than your raise, that isn't necessarily the truth.

This should also tell you that your supervisor will get recognition for the work done by his/her staff. That is because a supervisor is suppose to delegate work to his/her staff, and delegate in a way that results in all work being completed on time and all work being of high quality. That is what management is all about (at least one thing management is all about).

I remember doing an analysis of survey data while I worked for the Lower Manhattan Region of the New York Banking Division at Citibank. At the time, doing that analysis was not part of my normal responsibilities. However, Division (no, not Division from Nikita; Division here was the central management staff that presided over all the New York Banking Regions); was not interpreting the data from the surveys correctly, and in doing so, was putting my Region in a worse light than we should have been put in. My supervisor gave me permission to do the special analysis. When the analysis was a big hit with my Regional Business Manager, my boss was right there with me sharing in the praise. He did shine the light on me, but he received credit as well. And I agreed with that. After all, it was his call to let me do the special study.

There is also a side of your supervisor's job responsibilities that his/her staff often does not see. Supervisors are usually responsible for providing written status reports, explaining/implementing new company policies, managing his/her department's budget (money), training and developing his/her staff, managing the workplace, solving problems, analyzing the way work is being done to see if there are better ways to do it, providing support to other supervisors and senior management in the company, and much much more.

Your supervisor has little time, and no motivation to "be on your back for no reason." So again, if you think your supervisor is "out to get you", that will only be true if you are not performing to expected levels of work (quantity and quality), or are a disruptive force in the workplace.

Strategy for Meeting Supervisor's Expectations

There are steps you can take to consistently meet your supervisor's expectations. They are:

1. Accept the fact that your supervisor is control of your work life and treat him/her with respect at all times (when present, and when not there).
2. When told how the workplace operates, such as not taking your break at your work station (could appear to customers that you are available to them, could be disruptive to co-workers, etc.), abide by the rules of the workplace.
3. When given a task to do, do it to the best of your ability, and ask questions if you need help.
4. If you do not complete a task up to your supervisor's standards, take responsibility, do not blame others, and certainly do not blame your boss.
5. Take criticism well. Your supervisor is on your side and is only trying to help you (and his/her work unit), improve. It is not personal.

6. When you do something not up to standard (or wrong), show that you are eager to learn the better (right) way, and make the improvements (corrections) immediately.
7. Always keep your supervisor advised of what is going on, even if the message is not an easy one to tell him/her.
8. Do not get pig-headed. If your supervisor asks you try to do something a different way, give it a try with an all-out effort (not half-heartedly).
9. Always be honest with your supervisor. That includes conversations regarding work, the work environment, and by putting in an honest day's work on the job.
10. If you see something wrong, or if you see a way something can be done better, let your supervisor know, and then be willing to accept your supervisor's decision on how to proceed (do not argue or become stubborn or get an "attitude" because your idea was not used).

Meeting supervisor's expectations worksheet

Please classify the 10 steps listed for meeting supervisor's expectations as comes easy to me; understand it but need to work on it; or don't really see it will have to change my thinking, by placing the number of the statement in the appropriate comment category.

COMMENT	STATEMENT NUMBERS
comes easy to me	
understand it but need to work on it	
don't really see it will have to change my thinking	

Please indicate your plan of action for items in the "understand" or "don't really" categories:

____

____

____

____

____

____

____

____

____

____

____

Communicating with Supervisors

Communicating with supervisors is easy. In a way, many of us have been practicing since we were children. As a kid, your mom (and/or dad) was your supervisor.

When your mom told you how to do something, you were expected to do it that way or you risked being punished. The same is true with your supervisor. You have to be able to follow both written and verbal instructions. And not just follow most of the instructions, follow all of them. If at home you didn't follow all the instructions, you may have lost your radio/television/Internet/video game system/Xbox/cell phone rights depending upon the technology of your youth. At work you will get poor performance reviews which will lead to small pay raises (if any), and quite possibly losing your job.

That leads to the next step. If your mom (or dad) gave you instructions, and you didn't understand them and did them anyway and messed it up, it was back to a Stone Age day (no technology for you). You, hopefully, quickly learned to ask questions to avoid having to spend a boring night. It is the same when communicating with your supervisor. If you do not understand something, your supervisor will expect you to ask questions. So ask them to clarify everything you are not certain about regarding instructions (or anything else). Here is a great tip. When asking questions always have a pad of paper to write down what your supervisor is telling you when answering your questions. This is for two reasons. The first is that it will impress your supervisor that you are serious about doing a good job (positive personal signal). The second, and more important reason, is that while supervisors expect to be asked questions when their staff does not understand something; they do not like being asked the same questions over and over again by the same staff members. By writing down the answers, you will have notes to refer to in case you forget, and that could avoid you having to ask the same question to your supervisor a day or two (or week or two) later.

Try to minimize the number of times you need to interrupt your supervisor. Whenever possible, review an unfamiliar task in its entirety in advance of performing it so you can accumulate all of your questions and go to your Supervisor one time instead of a each time a question arises.

When you took a test in school, your mom (and/or dad) expected you to tell them your score on the test. If you got a bad score but told them, your consequences were usually less than if you hid the score from them and they found out on their own later. Worst case was when they got shocked by a bad grade on your report card because they did not know you were doing poorly. It is the same with your supervisor. Good or bad, you will be expected to communicate (verbally, or in writing) the results of your work. This may also include any obstacles you encountered while completing the work, and recommendations on how work procedures can be improved.

I don't know about you, but once in a while I'll call a customer service number to report a problem and a rude customer service phone representative will say something that he/she should not have said, and hang up. How foolish. I just call back because the problem still exists and report the comment and hang up. It is then very easy for that customer service phone representative's supervisor to find out who answered my call. So don't try to avoid difficult situations or tasks. Take them on.

Growing up at home, remember what happened if you answered the phone and forgot to give you mom or dad an important message? Right, you'd get "Flintstoned" again (no technology, back in the Stone Age). The same was true if you gave you mom or dad a message, but left out important details, such as the phone number of the person who called. Well, the same is true with your supervisor. Be sure to write down all messages for your supervisor accurately and completely, and give him/her all messages.

Following this advice to meet your supervisor's expectations, and communicating honestly and directly with your supervisor will go a long way in making you a very valuable employee to your employer.

Oh, and if you were one of those kids who got away with everything at home and avoided being punished, well your trip ends now. Your supervisor doesn't love you; doesn't look at you through the eyes of parent; and doesn't buy into the "my baby can do nothing wrong" crap. Thinking you can fool your supervisor is the perfect way to get fired, and end up jumping from entry level job to entry level job, never seeing your income grow.

EXERCISE PS6

Worker A was suppose to finish a report by the end of the day, however the analysis became more involved than initially thought. At day end, when Worker A goes to the Supervisor's office, the Supervisor is not in. Worker A, decides to go home, come in early and finish the report.

Q1. Is this good or poor communication? Why?

Worker A is given a new task. The new task comes with written instructions. At the very beginning of the instructions there is a contraction. Rather than going to the Supervisor's office to find out what should be done here, Worker A makes a note of the contradiction and continues to read the instructions, finding three more contradictions. Now with all four contradictions written down, Worker A knocks on the Supervisor's door.

Q2. Is this good or poor communication? Why?

*****

Understanding Expectations

One of the best ways to know what is expected of you on the job is to look at your job description. Job descriptions are documents that deal with a job position not an individual. Anyone who works in that job will be expected to perform the functions contained in the job description. This is important because at first you may only be expected to do some of those functions. Later when you are asked to do something new, you may be surprised, or upset, but if you had read your job description you would have known that the new function was part of the responsibilities for the job you were hired to perform.

This happens quite often. Work assignments are shifted; a new supervisor re-arranges how things operate, etc. Many workers feel that they are being asked to do something that they were not hired to do because they never read their job descriptions. Others may believe that the new task is more difficult so they should be paid more money. Usually, there was always a chance that these new, more difficult, work assignments were going to come their way. Depending upon the needs and staff size of the company, you may be called on to perform all or some of the tasks required of the job for which you were hired. Read your job description.

By the way, job descriptions can change. As new tasks, functions, products, technology, etc. are introduced into your workplace, job descriptions are revised to account for the new work. So you are not only hired to perform the tasks in the job description at the time you were hired; but to perform the tasks in your job description as it changes over time.

Performance Appraisals

Obtaining feedback on how well you are performing your job is a good thing, not a bad thing. One of the responsibilities of your supervisor is to generate a performance appraisal on you. How much money you get for a raise and your opportunities for a promotion to a job with more responsibility and more money are centered on your performance appraisal. Therefore, do not wait until your formal performance appraisal to see how well your supervisor thinks you are performing in your job. By obtaining feedback prior to your official appraisal, you will have time to correct issues before it becomes written into the records.

To do this, however, you have to be able to take criticism. If your supervisor tells you where you need improvement, he/she is doing you a favor. Yes, the criticism is a favor your supervisor is doing for you. By telling it to you in advance you can improve your job performance. If you do not get the criticism in advance, it will just come out anyway during the official performance appraisal.

Also keep this in mind. If your supervisor is not criticizing you, that means one of two things. It either means that your supervisor thinks you are perfect (congrats on that!), or that your supervisor believes that telling you what is wrong is meaningless because you are doing the best you can and cannot improve your performance (bummer!).

So you need to look at criticism the right way. That you are not the perfect employee (who is), and your supervisor believes in you (otherwise he/she won't bother to criticize you).

Personal performance appraisal pledge worksheet

If I have not had formal feedback from my supervisor during the last 6 months, I will ask my supervisor how well I am performing my job. Please initial _______

When my supervisor criticizes me, I understand it is to help me and I will not react poorly to that criticism. Please initial _______

After receiving criticism from my supervisor, I will generate a plan to improve my performance. Please initial _______

If I cannot think of a plan or need help determining how to improve my performance, I will ask my supervisor for his or her input or suggestions. Please initial _______

Ability to Handle Change

In many businesses, management and workplace procedures change often. You need to be able to adapt to these changes smoothly and without complaining. Remember, the goal for change is to improve the businesses profits, so that everyone can remain employed. Sometimes, however, there is a negative impact in the short run to get the long term benefit. In the NFL, a team may move away from a middle of the road veteran quarterback and insert a rookie with more long term potential. Often that leads to a worse record in year one (than if the team stayed with the middle of the road veteran), but bigger rewards down the line after the rookie gains experience and realizes his potential.

Therefore, do not get caught up in the idea that there is only one correct way to accomplish your tasks and to run your workplace; or that there is only one person who can manage you or your department.

If after giving new procedures time to see if they will work, you believe they are ineffective (not because it results in more or harder work for you, but that it is causing problems in the workplace or for customers); talk to your supervisor and explain why you believe the new procedures are causing problems. The key is talk, not argue. After getting your day in court, allow your supervisor to make his or her decision, and accept what he or she decides. In any event, embrace change, do not resist change.

Ability to Handle Stress

Many work environments are all about deadlines and employee productivity. Accept this as a fact, not a power trip from a power-hungry boss, or management trying to make life difficult for its employees. Deadlines and productivity measurements (used to track whether or not deadlines are on track to be met), are set to ensure that the company's customers remain satisfied and continue to do business with the company; or to keep costs in check. In either case the result is more profitability for the business which keeps everyone employed.

However, deadline-drive workplaces, at times, result in a hectic, stressful work environment. You need to be able to adapt. Most likely, the company you work for has been in business for awhile. Therefore, others have been able to meet the demands of the job, and thrive in the work environment. Look around you; I'm sure some of your current co-workers fit into that category. So if others have been able to adapt and succeed, you can too.

Business Basics

Since your ability to live your life and meet your life goals are tied very closely to the business for which you work; I thought it would be a good idea to write briefly about some basic business concepts. These are functions that most businesses undertake, either formally or informally.

Business Plan

A business plan is a living, breathing document that needs to be researched and written before a business starts. It contains strategies the business will follow and has projections for what it will cost the business to operate.

Not having a business plan is one of the main reasons businesses fail. Without a plan, it is difficult to know if the business is performing as expected, better than expected, or worse than expected.

The business plans I write for clients have the following sections:

1. Executive Summary
2. Industry - Historical Analysis
3. Industry - Current Trends
4. Industry - Conclusion
5. Strategic Plan

6. Marketing Plan
7. Management & Organization
8. Finances
9. Risks
10. Supporting Documents

The purposes of a business plan are:

- To look at the feasibility of establishing the business in the first place
- To set initial strategies so that management can track how the business is performing, so that, if needed, changes can be made in a timely manner
- To help the business owner determine his or her business strengths and weaknesses
- To get funding, whether a loan or an investor

Common Reasons Why Businesses Fail

Below is a list of common reasons why businesses fail. Some of the items on the list may help you better understand why management chooses to act as it does.

- No business plan
- Poor management
- No strategic planning process (a continuation of the business plan process)
- Undercapitalization (not enough money)
- Poor cash flow (money on hand to pay bills when they are due)
- Ineffective or nonexistent marketing
- Not knowing what competitors are doing
- Poor customer service
- The owner being a friend, not a boss to the employees
- Uncontrolled growth

Strategic Planning

Strategic planning is a four step process.

Step one is to generate a baseline strategy. SWOT analysis (business' strengths, weaknesses, opportunities, and threats) is a common tool to use for step one.

Step two is to develop a plan to:

- take advantage of/utilize strengths
- overcome/eliminate weaknesses
- find/capitalize on opportunities
- minimize/avoid/neutralize threats

A common process that is used to develop this plan is to generate a list of objectives, strategies, tactics and goals.

- Objectives are what you are trying to accomplish
- Strategies are the processes that will be implemented to accomplish the objectives
- Tactics are the specific steps that are needed to be done within each strategy
- Goals are specifics that need to be met to be assured of the success of the undertaking; without goals there would be no way to know if the strategies are accomplishing the objectives

Step three is to assign the tactics, with associated goals, to specific employees. Many times a tactic can involve multiple tasks. It is when these tasks are assigned to different people that team leaders are often required to help coordinate all the tasks. Sometimes that team leader can be a supervisor, sometimes a co-worker. Meeting the goals is often the basis for productivity and quality and timeliness measurements for individual workers and for work units, departments or the company as a whole.

Step four is to periodically review the progress and strategies and make adjustments and changes as needed.

Marketing

There are four main components to marketing:

- Price - this refers to the pricing strategy used by a business.
- Product - this refers to the full offering, not just the products and /or services sold to customers. For example: warranties, excellent customer service, money back guarantee, etc.
- Promotion - this refers to the tools used to inform customers and potential customers about the company's product and/or services. Promotion includes everything from commercials, to brochures, to web sites, to billboards, to blogs, to press releases, and more.
- Distribution - this refers to the methods and places where a company's products and services are delivered to its customers.

Sales

Sales drive businesses. Without sales, the business would not earn revenue, and therefore, would close. There are many different sales techniques and businesses often strategize on the best sales methods, sales approaches, and sales scripts to maximize closing sales. If you are in a sales position, and have your own approach, learn and try the company way first. You may pleasantly surprised at how well the company's sales process works.

A common phrase at many businesses is that everyone is a salesperson. What this means is that everyone will find him or herself in a position where they meet or know someone who could use their company's products or services. Therefore, be prepared. That means, at a minimum, have the contact information for someone in the company you can refer that person to.

However, since your economic health is tied to the success of the company you work for, you could be a little more proactive. This doesn't mean that you should aggressively go after sales. However, well informed entrepreneurs and sales people have what is called an elevator pitch.

An elevator pitch:

- Opens with a hook in the form of a statement or question that piques interest
- Consists of about 175 to 225 words that can be said in about 30 seconds
- Is spoken with passion and energy
- Ends by asking for something (a business card, a referral, an appointment)

You could development a stock answer to the question, "What do you do for a living?" that has a little bit of a sales twist. You can accomplish this by incorporating a little bit about the company's product and services into your answer, and conclude with, "I can give you the name and number of someone in the company who can help you if you like."

If you find out that the person you gave the contact information to does indeed call the company, don't be shy about informing your supervisor that it was you who pointed that customer to the sales department (or whoever's contact information you gave to the person with whom you were speaking).

EXERCISE PS7

Answer the following questions true or false

Q1. A business plan is important for all businesses.

Q2. If someone asks you about your company and job you should never bring up what your company sells and never give that person contact information for someone in your company.

Q3. Businesses need to goals so that they can determine whether or not their business strategies are working. This may mean measuring how much work you complete since the goals could be related to work completed.

Q4. If you and your fellow co-workers treat customers poorly, that could lead to the business failing.

Q5. As long as they are making some money on each product, it doesn't matter what price the company decides to charge on each product; profit is profit there is no strategy to setting prices.

*****

What if You Were the Boss

EXERCISE PS8

This whole chapter is an exercise. Please read what the follows and perform the exercise at the conclusion of the write-up.

Congratulations! You have just been promoted to Team Leader. Your Manager, Stuart Advocate, calls you into his office and has the following to say:

"As you know, we had to let go of Steve Oneyear. While production is okay there are too many signs that the workplace is deteriorating and we may lose our best workers. Since you have been taking management courses at night, I have decided to give you an opportunity to see if you can handle the job. In addition to your course work, your excellent work record in terms of job performance and attendance, and your ability to get along with your co-workers were major factors in my decision to offer you this opportunity. In fact, we are counting on your knowledge of your co-workers to fix the current problem. I suggest that you develop a plan of action for each worker to follow to ensure that the workplace will run smoothly so we can keep our best workers. Oh, by the way, production is fine, but not optimal. So while working on the plans of action, include recommendations for training assistance for each worker to help him or her become more productive in their job. If you develop a solid plan of action, and I see some improvement in 90 days, your promotion will become permanent. A 15% pay raise, the potential for bonuses and an additional paid week's vacation will come with the permanent promotion."

As you return to your work station you start thinking about the first five workers for whom you will develop a plan of action. You know them very well. What follows are your thoughts on these five employees:

Mike Dee

Mike is a very productive employee. He is also very well liked. Mike has a great sense of humor although at times Mike gets into arguments regarding some of his jokes. However, Mike does have a unifying effect on the team. He arranges and invites everyone out as a group to eat dinner once a month, and has gone to lunch with everyone in the group. Mike also takes pride in his work and the work for the unit as a whole; and his pride is contagious. Mike does, at times, come in late to work, but has never missed a deadline. However, while Mike's numbers on his reports are always accurate, he does not always highlight the key trends in his written analysis, and does not use charts and graphs in the report to help the reader visualize the trends easily. Therefore, Mr. Oneyear was constantly re-writing Mike's analysis, which may or may not have been the cause for some delays in other areas under Mr. Oneyear's control.

Josephina Prof

Josephina is the most productive employee on the team. She is single and attractive. While she does not go out of her way to socialize at work, there are often co-workers, almost always men, stopping by her desk trying to get into long conversations with her. She always tries to get rid of them quickly, so she can get back to work, but that isn't always successful. Two weeks ago, Josephina was called into Mr. Oneyear's office. Since then, she hardly even acknowledges her co-workers when they walk by, let alone talks to them. Because of the way Josephina is now treating her co-workers, you have overheard gossip "that Josephina now believes she's too good for the rest of us." In fact, one of them pointed out that "the only person Josephina has ever gone to lunch with is Mike Dee." A second chipped in, "Yeah, but that was only when she wasn't mad at him over one of his jokes." You happen to know she does go to lunch with co-workers other than Mike, since you had lunch with her just last week. Another rumor going around the office is that Josephina is looking for another job. You have a gut feeling that this one is true. Too bad you think; you would consider promoting her to your old job if she knew word processing.

Larry Lip

Larry is a good worker, but Larry is a party animal away from work. While Larry shows up on time and never calls in sick, it often takes him longer than his co-workers to get into his work assignments. His productivity is okay, but you know it could be better. Also, at times, it seems as though Larry just rolls out of bed and shows up for work. You know this because Larry has to work in close proximity to his co-workers and many have commented that Larry is wearing the same clothes as he was wearing the prior day. You can relate. Boy, how you hate working with Larry on those days. It's a challenge to the senses. In fact, you often thought about calling in sick on days where you were scheduled to work with Larry, but, of course you never did. But you begin to wonder if others had the same thought and actually do call in sick from time to time when scheduled to work with Larry. In addition, you are anticipating a problem with Larry. He has expressed a desire to advance in the company and has been taking the same management courses as you. You just know he will be disappointed that he didn't get the opportunity afforded you. Larry has also expressed interest in becoming Frankie Cash's back-up. However, Mr. Oneyear turned down his request to attend trade school because Larry would have to miss a half a day of work once a week for eight weeks to complete the training.

Jeannine Comeback

Jeannine is a new employee. She is married and has school-aged children at home. She demonstrates excellent potential and is fitting in well with the team. You have noticed that Jeannine does need to improve her computer skills to improve her overall job productivity. Jeannine was trained by Mr. Oneyear and often talked about how brilliant he was and how he knew the best way to do everything. Jeannine is also someone who writes down every step in a work procedure and performs those procedures while continually looking at her notes. You know you are going to make changes in how some of the tasks she just learned will be performed. You wonder if she will resist your changes. Another thing you noticed is that Jeannine is constantly going to the supply cabinet for new supplies. She seems to go through items such as pens, pencils, pads of paper, and scotch tape faster than anyone else. She is even on her second calculator and third pair of scissors. Knowing that if you get the promotion that you will be in charge of the budget, and therefore, held accountable for supplies, you wonder what's up with that.

Frankie Cash

Frankie has a highly specialized job and gets paid very well for his work. He does his work flawlessly. Due to the nature of his work, Frankie is the only worker required to wear safety equipment. Frankie often comments that he feels self-conscious being the only person walking around with gloves and a helmet. You have noticed that when Mr. Oneyear is not around, Frankie often worked without wearing his helmet. Frankie's skill is unique and there is no one else in the company who can perform his job. Mr. Oneyear, realizing this, often looked the other way when Frankie broke the rules. In fact, one time when Mr. Oneyear talked to Mike about coming in late in front of everybody in the room, Mike responded, "Hey, you don't get on Frankie when he comes in a half hour late so don't get on my back for coming in ten minutes late." Frankie is also very set in his ways and is not shy about speaking his mind on any topic, no matter who is around, no matter whether bringing up an inappropriate for the workplace topic from out of nowhere, or whether inviting himself into a private discussion. Often, after hearing Frankie's comments, you just shale your head and cannot believe the insensitive things Frankie says. And Frankie doesn't limit his comments to co-workers. On a couple of occasions he entered into uncomfortable conversations with customers. And Frankie's job contains no customer contact component. Frankie is also in the middle of the group that hangs around Josephina's desk.

Use the forms starting on the next page to record your detailed plan of action and training needs, for each employee. There is also a form to use for the topics you will cover in your first group meeting with these five employees (address the management change; discuss any items from the write-ups you believe should be brought up to the group). For the group meeting include the topic and a brief statement regarding the specifics you will cover on those topics.

Employee: Mike Dee

Training Plan

Plan of Action (what will you cover in your one-on-one meeting with Mike Dee)

Employee: Josephina Prof

Training Plan

Plan of Action (what will you cover in your one-on-one meeting with Josephina Prof)

Employee: Larry Lip

Training Plan

Plan of Action (what will you cover in your one-on-one meeting with Larry Lip)

Employee: Jeannine Comeback

Training Plan

Plan of Action (what will you cover in your one-on-one meeting with Jeannine Comeback)

Employee: Frankie Cash

Training Plan

Plan of Action (what will you cover in your one-on-one meeting with Frankie Cash)

Topics to cover in your first group meeting (a meeting with all 5 employees in attendance).

Include topics and brief write-up on the specifics to cover for each topic.

Certification Test Scenarios

People Skills Scenario 1

Another New Year, another set of New Year resolutions. However, this year will be different thinks Clara, this year I'm going to meet my work resolutions and get that promotion.

The job Clara is interested in is an important stepping stone for getting on the fast track to management. As Clara looks at the company organization chart she sees lots of people who have taken the same path she wants to take. Donna, head of Strategic Planning; the Marketing Director Rose, Head of Security, Martha; the Sales Manager Jack and his top salesperson Amy; and even the company nurse Rory; all held the position that Clara is interest in prior to getting their promotions.

So Clara starts to develop a formal work plan of action for the New Year. What follows are the items Clara put in her plan.

1. I often have to pass along bad information to customers from the big boss, The Doctor. The responses are often harsh so I need to learn not to take the negative reaction personally.

2. I have to stop going to my supervisor, asking questions when I am unsure of something. I'm smart. Instead I need to figure things out on my own.

3. I need to be more open to other people's ideas. I know I figure things out better than my co-workers (it is true that Clara figures things out better and well in advance of others), but that doesn't mean that they can't have good ideas too.

4. I need to be more careful to avoid office gossip. I never start the gossip, however, I did jump into the juicy conversation regarding whether Amy really liked the big boss, The Doctor, more than Rory. I know that much of the gossip got back to Rory, and he was hurt by all the talk and insinuation.

5. I need to be a better team player. When Jenny (a co-worker) was put in charge of the last project, I resented that I wasn't put in charge, and I didn't recognize her as someone who could assign me work, and judge my work, during the project. I thought I hid it well; I even looked her straight in the eye the whole time during our first long conversation, holding my head still.

6. I have a habit of constantly tapping my fingers, and I need to stop doing that because I think it gives people the wrong idea of what I am thinking.

7. I also have a habit of leaning forward slightly when I am interested in something; I think I may be giving the wrong impression there as well, so I need to be conscious to stop doing that as well.

8. I need to become a better team leader. The last time I was put in charge of a team, the following happened:

    a. I started off by telling the group about the project. I then wrote my ideas on the board and asked the group which tasks they would like to work on. After getting their feedback, I assigned roles to the team. Then I informed them what I expected of them, which included what each person needed to accomplish and the timeframes for accomplishing those tasks. I then invited them to the final presentation, which I gave myself. I stated the presentation by saying, "I want to thank management for giving me the opportunity to solve this important issue. I gave a lot of thought to this problem, and came up with a plan to fix it that I think you will all be very please with. I am very proud of the work I accomplished." When the presentation was done, and The Doctor asked who did the financials for the project, I responded, "Mickey did the reports."
    b. My lesson: I did a very good job, however next time I need to be sure that I get the proper credit. Therefore, I should have answered The Doctor's question, "I came up with the parameters, but Mickey crunched the numbers and typed the report."

9. I need to follow all the rules of the workplace. Eating lunch at one's desk is against the rules, so I need to stop doing that even though I'm not the only one who does it; and even though I do it to save time to get back to work faster.

10. I need to stand up for myself and stop cow-towing to my supervisor, River, when she criticizes me. I am the one doing the work, I know better than her if it is good or not. And I was right to tell her that I would try the new procedure she wanted, and then ignore it. I knew it wouldn't work.

11. I do, however, have to keep my supervisor, River, better informed. I need to let her know everything that is going on in a timely fashion. Maybe if I do that she will stop trying to give me better ways to do my job.

12. Since I have a good understanding of how the workplace operates, I need to let my supervisor know about some changes that I think will improve the entire operation, even in areas where others do the work. So I will tell her, and then I will follow whatever she thinks is best to do.

People Skills Scenario 2

Mike works for original Victory Corporation and, once again, it's that time of year. Boy time does fly; and now it's time for Mike's annual performance review once again.

However, much to his chagrin Mike discovers that it isn't his immediate boss Martin who will be giving him his performance review this year; it is the commander, herself, Diana who will be conducting this interview.

As Mike walks into her office, Diana stands and says, "I know I have a reputation as a very tough boss, but if you can at least recognize the things you did right and the things you did wrong this past year I won't "eat you alive," so to say.

Grasping his upper arms, Mike sits down.

The first topic Diana brings up is Mike's presentation to Juliet. During the presentation Juliet asked how many cases his department handled last year. Mike did not have the specifics but knew that it was somewhere between 3,500 and 7,500 cases. So Mike answered that his department handled 5,614 cases.

Next Diana brings up the strategic planning meeting between Mike and Ham. Ham is very set in his ways and is constantly arguing. But the meeting between Mike and Ham went well with no arguments. Diana then asks him how he was able to accomplish that. Chin up, Mike starts to answer; "I started with a strategy to concentrate on what I knew we agreed on first, to get us on the same page and eliminate arguments right off the bat."

Diana then asks if Mike's son ever left the cult he joined. She further adds to Mike that it's a shame that you have to be careful not to let him know how bad you believe the cult leader is. Mike responds, how did you know about that? Diana answers; "Are you kidding; who in the company haven't you talked to about this?"

Diana then follows up that rhetorical question by asking Mike, "Do you have any issues with Victory Corporation?" Mike responds, "Why would you ask that?" Diana says, "Do you think I don't know what goes on in my workplace? I wish if you had complaints that you would bring them up with your supervisor Martin, or me; not discuss them with your co-workers." Stroking his nose, and in a tone similar to Sansa Stark when talking about her pending marriage to King Joffrey in *Game of Thrones*, Mike says, "I have never complained to my co-workers about Victory Corporation."

Diana then says, "Let me lighten the mood a bit. Tell me about the situation with Willie that happened a few months back." Mike then responds, "I saw that Willie was placing products in storage bins before labels where placed on them. I knew that if the labels were missing the wrong products could be shipped to the wrong clients and that could cost the company money, result in customer dissatisfaction, and lost accounts. So I spoke to Willie who then started putting the labels on before putting the products into storage bins. Diana followed up by saying, "Willie doesn't work for you. In fact he is in a different department." Mike, said, "That's right, but I used to do that job so I knew the correct procedure. Boy you really do see all." "Yes" said Diana, "My eyes are the eyes of an eagle."

Next up, Diana asked Mike about the time he was put in charge of the Project Resistance. Diana commented that she was at the oral presentation of the findings, and would Mike please explain to her how he decided on the strategy for the presentation format. Mike answered, "I wanted everyone involved in the project to have a role in the presentation, so that management would be aware of their contributions. After all, it was team effort. However, I wanted to start the presentation to talk about our process and challenges; and then I wanted to conclude the presentation presenting the team's solutions since I was the Team Leader."

Knowing that there were a lot of changes that took place during the year; Diana asks Mike, "How did all the changes impact you?" Mike responded, "The changes really helped. The process is running more smoothly, there are fewer work stoppages and errors. In addition, I loved learning the new process."

Diana said, "Last topic. I know you are new to the Science Frontiers account. Their CEO, Nathan, can be tough to deal with. How are you holding up? I know our prior two account managers for Science Frontiers thrived in the role, but I know with the tight deadlines, the high employee productivity needed to meet those deadlines, and no-errors-allowed policy, that account can be highly stressful." Mike answers," I'm very glad you recognize that. That account is keeping me up at night. You know what would help, though; do away with all those Quality Assurance people looking over my shoulder. I feel enough pressure without being told if my productivity is falling behind, or my last batch had an error."

After Mike informs Diana what he did right and what he did wrong regarding these situations, Mike walks back to his desk waiting for his written performance appraisal to see if he identified his good workplace actions and his mistakes correctly.

The Author's Training Philosophy

When I was hired to develop a work readiness curriculum in 2002 there were already a number of established work readiness training programs. With employers complaining about the lack of job skills and poor workplace behaviors by their employees in focus groups throughout the United States, I knew I had to develop more than a training curriculum; I needed to create a better way to deliver workplace training.

First, let's look at traditional programs.

Traditional Programs

Practically all workplace training programs follow models used in education. That means that they are assessment based. FCAT, SAT, etc., determine success in education and, similarly, a certification test determines success in many workplace training courses. And once workplace training ends there is no formal process to hold the individuals trained accountable for what they learned during training.

In fact, assessment tests have become so important in education that schools not only teach students knowledge, but teach students how to take tests. They must. After all, funding is often tied to their students' performances on tests such as the FCAT. Certainly many high school juniors and seniors enroll in courses to help them learn how to improve their SAT scores. And this is not just the case with kids. How many construction management schools, real estate schools, and even schools to help with the BAR exam for attorneys are out there? These schools often teach their students how to take and pass tests.

What does this mean? It means that if a student truly knows only 55% of the required knowledge, but can reduce the other questions to a possible 1 in 3 choice, the laws of probability conclude that the student's expected result on the test is 70%.

Even worse, if a student truly knows only 60% of the required knowledge, but can reduce the other questions to a possible 1 in 2 choice, the laws of probability conclude that the student's expected result on the test is 80%. That means a student whose knowledge base is an "F" (60% was failing grade when I went to school), appears to be a "B" student.

While educators cling to the argument that assessment tests are good indicators of success, no one can make that case when dealing with job skills and behaviors. As an example let's use the following multiple choice question:

If you wake up in the morning and your car will not start, you should:

A) Have made prior arrangements with a coworker who lives in your neighborhood to serve as an emergency ride to work.

Whether because of actual knowledge or eliminating answers like, "B) Take as many days off of work as you need to get your car fixed," someone answering this question correctly does not mean that that is the behavior he or she will follow if this situation actually happened to him or her. Workplace training is NOT about answering questions correctly. It's about doing the right thing in the workplace. That is accomplished through training materials that not only teach what is expected in the workplace, but ***why*** that skill/behavior is important in the workplace; and also uses real life examples that everyone can relate to outside of the workplace to help illustrate key points. In workplace training, it is the journey (curriculum) that is the key, not the final destination (assessment test). This is because success is measured in the attitudes changed and instilled in participants, not on how much work readiness knowledge they possess.

While this may be obvious to you and me, it isn't obvious to the powers that be. For example, instead of investing in a structured program with an effective curriculum that would produce high-quality employees that employers could rely on; many states either independently or in groups decided to spend funds on generating work readiness credentials through assessment testing. They appear to care more about formulating the perfect question, than the perfect learning tool.

Work readiness certification test results from programs that do not have effective curriculum that changes and shapes attitudes, are, at best, an indicator for possible success and, at worst, a false hope for the business community that hires the "credentialed graduates."

Jay Goldberg's Workplace Training Philosophy

I have been developing and fine-tuning my workplace training program and philosophy since 2002. What follows is a list of the key components for what I know is the correct way to implement a workplace training program.

(1) The client for employee training programs is the **business community** first, and the classroom participants second. Why? Employers observing the participants in the workplace will ultimately determine if the training program is successful; not

how well the participants perform in class or on tests. In addition, if employers like the program and believe they can rely on the participants who successfully complete the training to perform well in the workplace; they will value, hire and promote graduates of the program. And that is the main reason the participants are taking the training; to get jobs, keep jobs, and grow in their jobs. In other words, participants want to increase their value to employers.

This realization separates the training programs developed and implemented by the author from most of the other programs in the marketplace. Schools (for sure) and most other venues as well, take on the strategy to improve their students as much as possible, and then market them as vigorously as they can to the marketplace. The result is often graduates, who the school/ training venue expect may fall short of expectations, getting hired and, in fact, falling short of expectations. This result hurts future graduates of the program.

Therefore, my workplace training programs do not allow participants to achieve full certification unless they demonstrate that the main client (the business community) will be able to rely on them at work.

(2) A curriculum that not only teaches what is expected, but why that skill/behavior is important in the workplace, and uses real life examples that everyone can relate to outside of the workplace to illustrate key points, is the foundation to having a successful workplace training program. By clearly defining important workplace skills and behaviors, and informing participants why those skills and behaviors are important to employers; the program sets a baseline of understanding and helps change the participants' attitudes and behaviors.

(3) The training needs to be run like a place of business not a typical educational classroom. The instructor is not just the trainer, but during training is the supervisor, and the participants treat each other as co-workers, not training buddies or friends.

(4) After taking workplace training courses, exams (certification exams or otherwise) are used NOT to indicate competency, but to demonstrate that the participants understood the concepts taught during training so that their employers can start holding them accountable for demonstrating those competencies on the job.

(5) Since performance on the job is what is important to employers, the key program assessments are not the exams, but demonstrated competencies the participants prove every day in class. This also helps the participants understand how they will be evaluated on the job. As an example, during training, a participant demonstrates the ability to not be tardy by never being late to a training session and never extending breaks during a training session.

(6) Since certified program graduates will have shown that they understand the concepts taught during training, and that they can follow some simple, basic rules that are employed during training (through demonstrated competencies); employers should be encouraged to incorporate the competency statements in the training program into their employees' formal performance appraisals.

(7) Within the training program, all competency statements must be very well defined. There should be no leeway given to individual trainers in scoring pass/fail on competencies.

(8) Hold the participants accountable for meeting all their competencies. Recommend to the employers you work with to help place your graduates, that they tie individual compensation (raises, bonuses, etc.) and individual/work unit rewards (employee of the month, monthly pizza party, etc.) to their employees' performances in meeting their competencies.

(9) In addition to training participants, if there are multiple people giving the training sessions, there needs to be a consistent approach between all trainers. That means there may need to be train-the-trainer sessions to ensure all trainers conduct their training in a consistent manner. This is especially true given that the participants will be held accountable for implementing what they learn in the training session every day on the job. Knowing that everyone was trained the same way provides role models who completed the program, were hired, and are now succeeding in the workplace. And since these former program participants received the exact same training as the current participants, there are no excuses for the current participants to fail once they enter the workplace. Program consistency between trainers means no former graduate will be ale to use the excuse, "my instructor never taught me that" to their employer who hired them because of their work readiness credential.

(10) As you can see my program philosophy is very intricate and everything must work in concert to ensure optimal success. Therefore, in addition to instructor training there must be instructor audits to ensure that all teachers/trainers are following and teaching the program correctly.

Jay Goldberg's Background in Work Readiness

As mentioned previously, in 2002 I was hired to develop a work readiness curriculum that I grew into a work readiness philosophy and program. The program I developed was called the best work readiness certification program in the United States by a member of the National Skills Standard Board at a presentation of the Program in Jacksonville, Florida on 01/13/03.

The results from my initial client far exceeded those of other work readiness programs. Employers lined up to hire the graduates and found that over 85% of the graduates remained employed six months later, and over 30% received promotions.

Later I modified and added to the program for a second client.

Since that time I wrote a well-reviewed work readiness book for individuals titled, *How to Get, Keep and Be Well Paid in a Job* (Outskirts Press, ISBN: 9781432725297).

Now I have constructed a four module work readiness and customer service training program that can be used in teaching venues and for on the job training. The four modules each come with recommended competencies and a final online certification test (to use as proof of knowledge so that these individuals can now be held accountable for demonstrating what they leaned every day at work). Participants should have to pass all of the competencies in order to be eligible to sit for the certification test.

About the Author

Jay Goldberg, MBA, is a former Service Director for Citibank. At Citibank, Mr. Goldberg specialized in customer service management, measurement, training, capacity planning, profitability, MIS reporting, and strategic planning.

After almost fourteen years with Citibank, Mr. Goldberg left to form his own consulting firm, DTR Inc. DTR Inc. specializes in writing business plans, developing workplace training programs, designing and implementing customer service strategies, performing strategic planning and market research (e.g., surveys, focus groups, etc.), helping businesses build their brands, and training managers and employees.

At DTR Inc., Mr. Goldberg developed the program parameters, program strategy, curriculum, lesson plans, assessments, competency statements, and certification tests for a Work Readiness Training Program called the best Work Readiness Certification Program in the United States by a representative of the National Skills Standard Board at a presentation of the Program in Jacksonville, Florida on 01/13/03.

Mr. Goldberg later updated, modified and added to that Program for a second client and wrote a book, "How to Get, Keep and Be Well Paid in a Job" (ISBN = 9781432725297), specifically tailored to individuals looking to improve their work readiness skills.

In 2007, Mr. Goldberg was instrumental in helping the Palm Beach County Resource Center develop a revolutionary Entrepreneurship Training Program. The program's structure was unlike any other in the marketplace, and would prove to be highly successful.

In 2012, Mr. Goldberg's entrepreneurship book, "Building a Successful Business," (ISBN = 9781470000639) was published. The book is now being used as a textbook for entrepreneurship courses. The book is both a textbook and a workbook with tools entrepreneurs can use to help start, grow and manage their businesses.

While at the Palm Beach County Resource Center, Mr. Goldberg worked with hundreds of small businesses and got a good handle on how to best structure and implement a work readiness training program to ensure that the benefits of training would be demonstrated in the workplace.

In 2013 Mr. Goldberg published his book for his comprehensive work readiness and customer service training program. There is a teacher book, a classroom book (without answers) and PowerPoint presentations available in the full program.

Contact Mr. Goldberg at Book@DTRConsulting.BIZ. Be sure to write "your work readiness book" in the subject line to ensure that your email is not deleted as junk mail. His business's web site is www.DTRConsulting.BIZ.

Rock Trees: The Beatles: Volume 1: The Paul McCartney Tree

By JAY GOLDBERG

ISBN = 9781494739102

Six Degrees of Separation was originally proposed by Frigyes Karinthy. The theory says that everyone in the world can be connected through a maximum of six steps. Applying that theory to The Beatles, this book shows how 1,550 bands/artists connect back to The Beatles.

This is Volume One of a planned series and examines the Paul McCartney "Rock Tree." The other Beatles will get their own books in the future.

The book contains fifty "rock trees" each with thirty one bands/artists per tree and each with a companion chart showing how the bands are connected.

The goal was not to repeat any band/artist, although musicians can be solo artists and parts of different bands. I accomplished that goal.

Only band members or guest or studio musicians or singers were used to connect the bands/artists. Song writing, production, engineering, etc. credits did not count.

FOR MORE INFORMATION VISIT

www.createspace.com/4580254

www.ingramcontent.com/pod-product-compliance
Lightning Source LLC
Chambersburg PA
CBHW070840180526
45168CB00002B/902